Focused on the Coast

The photographic work of Neal Parent

Published by WoodenBoat

All inquiries should be sent to:
Parent Gallery
92 Main Street
Belfast, Maine 04915
www.nealparent.com

Front Cover: Fishing the Banks

Photography: Neal Parent

Book Design: Lindy Gifford

Published by WoodenBoat Publications
Naskeag Road, PO Box 78
Brooklin, Maine 04616 USA
207-359-4651
www.woodenboat.com

Printed in China by Regent Publishing

Parent, Neal.
    Focused on the coast : the photographic work of Neal Parent.
        p. cm.
    ISBN 0-937822-74-4 (alk. paper)
    1. Marine photography. 2. Seashore in art. I. Title.

TR670 .P365 2002
779'.37'092—dc21
                                        2002028876

This book is dedicated to Joanne, Brian, Elisha and Alexander.
Follow your dreams.

Neal Parent's black-and-white photographs, spaced along the walls of his gallery in Belfast, Maine, reflect the artist as well as his art. They are the work of a man who loves the Maine coast, the people who make a living along its shore, and the creatures that inhabit the natural world. His images engage the viewer and remain embedded in the mind's eye.

Neal's subjects are as diverse as his interests. The warmth of *A mother's kiss* stands in sharp contrast to the deck of a Banks fishing vessel in a storm-tossed sea, or the grace of a great blue heron as it lifts off the water, its feet trailing a line of crystal beads on the surface. Nothing is static. All are absorbed with the immediacy of the moment.

The Parent Gallery is the culmination of twenty-five years of photography that has gained national recognition. An aura of light and space has prevailed here since it opened in 2001 on a corner of the main street in this seacoast town. A small framed letter from Ansel Adams on the counter notes that he "had photographed in Maine and it was a difficult place to capture." He added that Neal had "done a fine job of capturing the essence of Maine."

It is this "essence of Maine" that Neal conveys in his photographs, an absorbing insight into the character of a place. "I'm fascinated by everything, and I shoot the way I see it." Never without his camera, he is drawn to extremes of weather in all seasons. With the temperature at 15 below at dawn on Belfast Harbor, he could barely move his fingers as he caught the beauty of sea smoke rising behind an ice-sheathed shrub. His photo, *Crystal morning*, is one of the most ethereal images in the gallery.

One winter night, Neal let out his dog and was fascinated by shadow patterns under the village streetlight. He grabbed his camera and made a minute-and a-half time exposure for *Streetlight design* before realizing he was knee-deep in snow in his stockinged feet.

The stark simplicity of his photo *Wind-shaped* sets it apart from the rest of the exhibit. Black line-thin reeds bent above their rippled reflection in the water often suggest Picasso to some viewers.

Neal has always worked with 35mm cameras. He prefers to photograph with natural light, without filters, and he processes and prints his own film. "Only the photographer is the one who remembers what he saw at the time the shutter was depressed. Only he can bring out in his prints what he wants to convey." With thirty years of darkroom experience, he has mastered the challenging process of printing 40-inch prints from 35mm negatives.

It is unusual for a photographer of Neal's stature to work with only two cameras—a 35mm Canon F1 and a Canon EOS 1. He shoots with Kodak Tri-X film and uses a variety of lenses—20-300mm, a 28-135mm, and a 75-300mm. He particularly likes his stabilizer lens with a gyro that locks in to counter the roll aboard a boat.

He didn't own a gyro, but wished he did, when he shot the cover photo, *Fishing the Banks*. He was aboard a trawler out of New Bedford during a ten-day trip 200 miles at sea on Georges Bank. On assignment for the *National Fisherman*, he prayed for a little action going out. When we ran into forty-foot seas, "I said, 'Okay, Lord, that's enough.' They'd have thrown me over the side if they knew." It was so rough that Neal tied himself to a pole to keep his balance as the sea washed over the deck. He shot his photos with his head and camera in a plastic bag, through a hole cut for the lens. During that trip, he frac-

tured his wrist and broke a lens. "I was scared, but I'd do it again in a heartbeat." On the return trip, Neal continued to tie himself to the upright for photographs, including his on-deck shot, *Riding out the storm*.

Neal's love of the coast and the workaday lives of its people took root while he grew up on Cape Cod. But he was married with two small children before he ever held a camera. He excelled in art all through high school and planned to continue art study in Boston when he graduated. Instead, he went into the service during the Vietnam War, finding himself stationed most of the time at the Strategic Air Command in Omaha, Nebraska. He was always sketching—serious subjects, cartoons, anything as an outlet for his creative ability. The commanding officer, impressed by his talent, assigned him to do a special three-month art project at the base.

Neal and Linda Gavin were married in 1967 while he was in the Air Force. They were both twenty and had known each other since they were twelve. After the service, he went to work as an illustrator for the *Orleans Oracle*, his home-town paper. A short time later, he was shifted to the darkroom, totally unfamiliar with the process. With characteristic ingenuity, he learned on the job, leaving three years later as a skilled professional.

On a camping trip to Katahdin, Neal and Lin stopped at a campground on the outskirts of Camden. He had been to Katahdin with the Boy Scouts when he was a kid but had never seen the Maine coast. "I loved every second of it. That's how I fell in love with this state."

On their way home from Katahdin, they stopped in Camden again. Out of curiosity, Neal checked out the *Camden Herald's* help-wanted ads, and there it was—an ad for a darkroom technician. "It was ironic," he recalls, when he saw the *Herald's* cellar darkroom. "It was just like the place I'd worked in for three years." Negatives hung from clothespins on a wire stretched across the room under a fluttering fluorescent light. Bound copies of 100 years of the *Camden Herald* gathered dust on shelves against the bare stone walls. It had character, and it was cool on a hot summer day.

Neal didn't need a job; he had just started his own house-painting business. But the pull of the Maine coast was too strong. When he received word from the *Herald*, where I was editor, that he was hired, he gave notice to his partner, threw his tent and some clothes into the family Ford, and came to Maine to start work and find a place to live.

It was raining when he arrived, and the campground was wet. He assured me he'd be fine—he just needed to borrow some pots and pans. Neal was on the job the next morning, and he slipped into the usual press-day chaos as though he were home.

With all his technical and artistic ability, Neal had never used a camera, but it was a matter of expediency for everyone on the small *Herald* staff to take news and feature photos. He soon became familiar with the various cameras in the office—Nikkormat, Minolta, and a Honeywell-Pentax he got in trade for barnbuilding labor. When the Honeywell-Pentax was stolen from his car, he bought a Minolta and later sold it for a good buy on a 35mm Canon.

With the camera, Neal found the perfect release for his creative expression. From then on, he was never without it. He could duck out the darkroom door to the harbor while his prints were drying and shoot a roll of film on the schooners, lobstermen, and bench-sitters on the wharf.

"I could sit on a park bench and watch people all day," he once said. "You get pretty close to people if you watch them, talk to them, and take their pictures." This rapport with people breathes life into his photographs. The faces of women gossiping at town meeting, and an old yacht captain in paint-splattered overalls at a local lunch counter, convey a rooted human character in the commonplace. As months went by, these, among scores of Neal's photos that appeared weekly in the *Herald*, attracted an admiring public. Many were included in his first book, *My Corner of Maine*, published in 1982 by Down East Books. Seven years later, Down East published his second book, *Neal Parent's Maine*.

In this collection, 98 percent of the photographs were taken in Maine, the rest elsewhere in New England. A spring mist rising on a pond in Connecticut forms the backdrop for three swans in *Morning ritual*, taken at the moment the male spread his wings in a dramatic performance, perhaps to attract the two females. Here, as with people, setting is integral to Neal's photographs. He sees the picture before he picks up his camera; he anticipates the action and shoots quickly, making different exposures.

This book includes a photo of Phil Raynes, long a favorite character in Camden Harbor, as he rows his lobster traps to the dock stern-to, because, as he'd answer curious tourists, "I like to see where I'm going." A few miles inland, he photographed a reclusive woodsman at his camp, where he finds his Maine "The Way Life Should Be."

Neal has an innate ability to convey a human presence in the inanimate. *Signs of the times* focuses on the front end of an abandoned school bus with a 1967 Maine license plate. But the small Scientology emblem screwed on the cracked fender rouses curiosity about the owner.

An expectant atmosphere prevails in the vacant interior of a boathouse where pot buoys hang from the rafters, coils of line fill a corner, and plank-bottomed chairs stand near an electric heater. The dartboard propped against one wall and the cribbage board, left in play on the table, await the nightly gathering of lobstermen on Monhegan island.

In 1980, Neal was invited to exhibit his photographs at Camden's annual outdoor Arts and Crafts Show. He and Lin borrowed money to mat and frame prints and set up a booth, half fearful that nothing would sell. Instead, people crowded his booth all day, bought all his photos, and placed orders for more. Encouraged by the response, he decided to enter more shows. For the next twenty years, he and Lin traveled from Maine to Florida and west to Columbus, Ohio, forty weekends a year, often sleeping in their van, to exhibit at major juried shows where his photographs won countless awards.

Another dimension opened for Neal in early September 1982, when Captain Alan Talbot invited him aboard his schooner *Roseway* for a week. Neal shot rolls of film—harbors crowded with fishing boats, spruce-crowned islands, granite headlands, villagers trading on the wharves. When passengers with high-priced equipment began asking for help with their own cameras, Neal realized he could teach a photography class aboard the *Roseway* for one week each season. Captain Talbot agreed.

Back on shore, teaching a boatload of passengers seemed more formidable. Neal persuaded Carol Sebold, a friend and local artist, to teach a watercolor class aboard the schooner the same week. "Artists Under Sail" was launched the following season. For the next fifteen years, including two in the Virgin Islands, that week was the highlight of the *Roseway's* season. Passengers returned year after year, and scores became good friends. When the *Roseway* was retired, Neal and Carol continued their classes for another five years aboard the Camden-based ketch *Angelique*, with Captain Mike McHenry.

"You've got to make it fun," Neal would tell his class. "You're here to enjoy yourselves. I'd kid with them. Tell them there are no bad questions. If they miss something, put their hand up." An entertaining mimic and exceptional harmonica player, Neal made his schooner classes lively as well as productive.

One of his most dramatic night photos, *Midnight on the wharf*, was taken when the *Roseway* anchored in Stonington. A light on the pier casts its moonlike image on the water and reflects the face of a weathered shack and boats tied at the float. Neal processed all his students' film aboard the schooner in makeshift quarters. The week ended with an often-hilarious slide show of student work and a skit by Neal and Carol.

During schooner weeks, Neal liked to row ashore to photograph before passengers were awake. One morning at Winter Harbor on Vinalhaven, he arrived as the first rays of sun reflected in the water the image of a wooded point and the masts of two schooners anchored in the cove. Cloud reflections dapple the calm surface. The peace and serenity of the scene prevails in his photo *How still the morning*.

Neal was teaching his one-week course in marine photography at the WoodenBoat School during the annual schooner rendezvous week when he took the last photo in this book. It shows a silhouetted figure on the flag draped stern deck of the Camden schooner *Mary Day* at sunset, September 11, 2001. All the schooners gathered that day fired their cannons at 7 p.m. As stillness settled over the fleet, Capt. Ken Barnes, of the Rockland schooner *Stephen Taber*, played "Amazing Grace" on his bagpipe. "All my students had tears in their eyes."

Fog, a fact of life along the coast, creates subtle as well as startling effects for a photographer. Neal was aboard the *Angelique* when the three-masted *Victory Chimes* ghosted out of a fogbank nearly bow to bow with a lobsterboat coming out of Bass Harbor—a near-miss he terms *Rush hour in Maine*.

One of the annual Great Schooner Races produced *Wing on wing*, an unusual shot of the entire fleet, "Wing on Wing", with the venerable Camden schooner, *Grace Bailey* in the lead. A close-up of the century old vessel on a port tack is titled, *Grace Bailey—one hundred years of sailing*.

The gallery frees Neal from the arduous exhibition trail. He limits his teaching to private classes at his Belfast studio for three students a week during spring and fall. They come from all over the country and abroad, some year after year. Lin manages the gallery operation and shares gallery hours with Neal and their daughter, Joanne, a talented watercolorist and pastel artist. She maintains her own exhibit in an area of the Parent Gallery.

Joanne and her brother, Brian, are both licensed captains. Brian is based in Newport, Rhode Island. Joanne sailed with her husband while he captained an ocean-going yacht. Elisha, the youngest, served a year on the two-masted privateer *Lynx*, advancing to senior deckhand. Later assigned to engine care, she learned enough to spark an interest in studying mechanics.

Neal continues to focus his lens on Maine. His black-and-white photographs capture the rugged beauty of its land and the independent spirit of its people, a living portrayal of the character of a place.

—Jane Day

It has been twenty-seven years since Jane Day, then editor of the weekly *Camden Herald*, gave me a camera and said, "Go ahead, see if you can get some shots." Having already spent the previous three years developing film and printing photographs for reporters, I had a basic idea of what should be done. The very first roll produced a few images that were selected for that week's issue of the paper—the seed had been planted! After that, regardless of the weather, sunny or stormy (preferably stormy), I would be out shooting. I established a close relationship with the camera—an attachment that has continued to this day.

My training had been in commercial art—painting or drawing, it didn't matter, as long as I was creating something. The camera has been an outlet for that side of me that needs to be creative. I learned by trial and error and still continue to learn, realizing that in this particular field there will be no end. There will never be a point when I can say I know all there is to know about photography. I am pleased, for no matter how much technology attempts to simplify photography, it remains a challenge to all who pursue it. I have a quote from somewhere that says, "Photography is no simpler than any other art form, nor is it more complicated. Ultimate achievement taxes the capacity of the artist whatever his medium may be." I believe this to be true. For me, taking the photograph is the sketch; developing and printing the image is the completion of the art form.

This collection of images is drawn from my fascination with the coast and its inhabitants. Growing up on Cape Cod and now living on the Maine coast has kept that fascination alive. Whether several hundred miles at sea in a storm, or sitting in a fishing shack watching sea smoke rise off the cold winter ocean, the connection is there. I love the sea and anything to do with it. My students repeatedly ask what they should look for regarding subject matter. Perhaps my answer sounds corny, but I advise them to shoot with their heart as much as their eyes. If something they see stirs an emotion within, then it probably will be reflected in their finished image.

Looking through over a quarter of a century's worth of negatives in order to select images for this collection was a challenge. To select only the more dramatic photographs I display in galleries would have been the easy route. I wanted, however, to reflect those moments that stirred some particular emotion in me... the moment in high seas with the water breaking over the rail, the moment of solitude as a dory seems to be floating in the thick morning fog or the moment when the old sailor leaned on the boathouse door smoking his pipe pondering days gone by. These moments were more than simply pretty scenes. They offered to me spontaneous inspiration through an instant of unique lighting, my feelings varying from complete tranquility to powerless admiration.

The ocean has been and always will be a magnet for me. I am drawn to the coast constantly whether it is calm or storm. To be able to share these individual moments with others is incredibly rewarding. Although reactions to each image may be completely different than mine; my hope is they may feel what I did when looked the through lens and hit the shutter.

—Neal Parent

Nighttime in Stonington

Maine—the way it is cracked up to be

Focused on the Coast

Roseway leads

Ascension

Full throttle

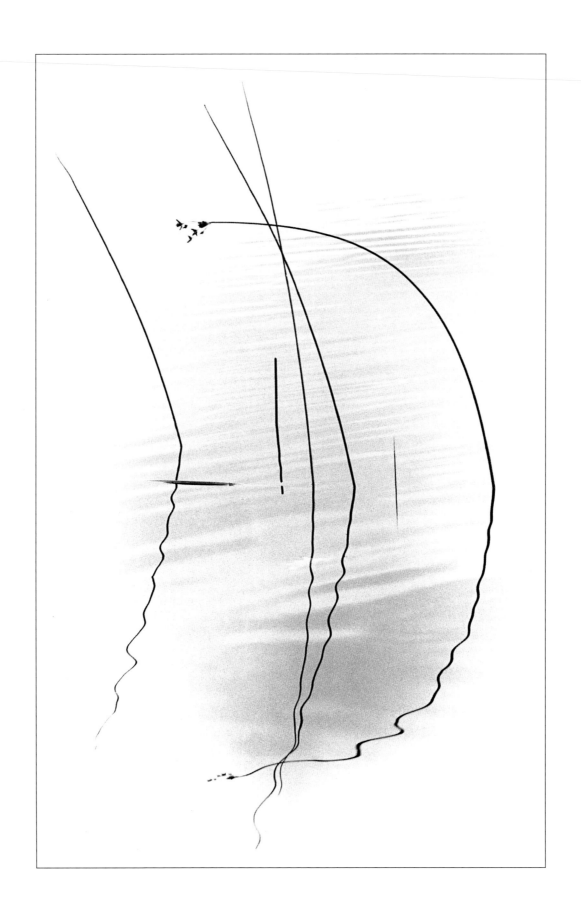

Wind-shaped

Where soldiers stood

Midnight on deck

How still the morning

The *Timberwind* closes the gap

Natural frame

Mending the nets

Lobster trap cat

Conditional reflection

The fishermen's shack

Night vigil

Lookout's aloft

Grace Bailey—one hundred years of sailing

Sunset, Isle au Haut

Homeward bound

Riding out the storm

One summer's night

Shadows of love

Racing to the mark

Signs of the times

January's pasture

Captain Dan Pease

Take care of your bottom

Time to ponder

Getting ready for spring

Heading to work

Puffin aerobics

The 12½ line up

Going to the maul

No more to go out

Training them young

Fogbound sentinel

Day of the storm

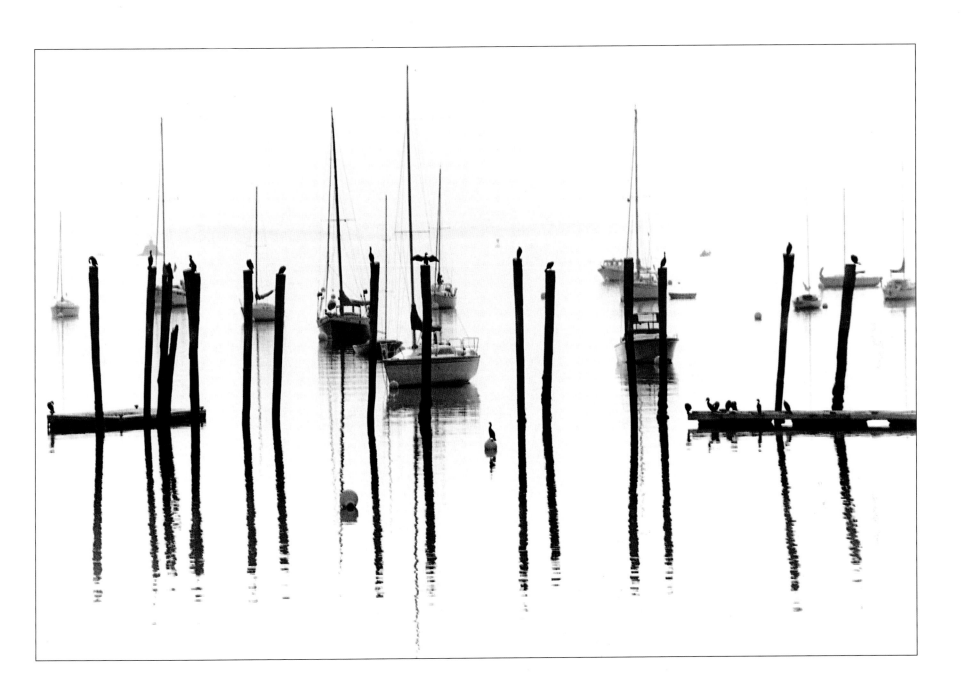

Harbor silhouettes

The passage, five days out

Halfway up the forestay

Hauling out the traps

No day to sail

Reaching safe harbor

Mackerel skies

All right, Simon says…

Maine—the way life should be

Winter along the shore

Christmas morning

Racing across the bay

Bringing in the nets

Island light

After the hurricane

Freedom

Icebound and heavy

A mother's kiss

Seasons end

Barely visible

Working on the *Stephen Taber*

Reflecting on the past

Fishing the Banks

Hard work

Burying the rail

Piping at dusk, 9 -11-2001

Ocean delight

Cappy does a winter touch up

Approaching storm

Foggy reflections

Life on the rocks

In the lead

Stormy departure

Heeled over

Along the Maine coast

Midnight on the wharf

Afternoon at the Chip-and-Cuss Shop

Launching the *Whitefin*

Nor'easter

The bait house

Hazy days graze

Rush hour in Maine

Under the bowsprit

Hauling traps

Liftoff

Streetlight design

Shamrock

Good stuff's on the bottom

The *Spirit of Unity*

Coastal dawn

Pouring the keel

The *Mercantile*

Dawn, Block Island

When there's no wind, row

Captain Ted Schmidt

How dry I am

Sail shadows

Foggy crossing

Portland Head Light

Dawn solitude

Hauling in the nets

Securing the float

On fog watch

Waiting

Heading home

The raft-up

To the windward side

Peaceful

The lobsterman

Lowering the topmast

Midwinter run

Dipping the boom

Head of the harbor

Foggy departure

Downeast dawn

Harbor concert

The *Angelique*

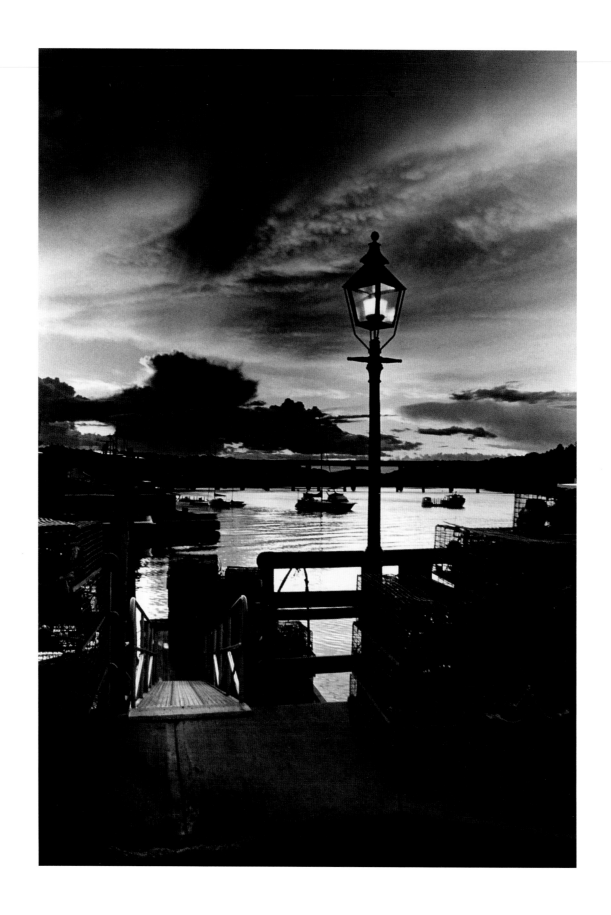

Day's end

Racing towards the mark

A reflecting adventure

Morning ritual

Captains Ellen and Ken Barnes

Maine skies

Ice bound

Good day for chowder

Morning coffee

The *Heritage* races in

The No Name Storm begins

Life is a good footrope

Wildhorses maiden sail

Captain Miles goes ashore

Ahh, that's the spot

Crystal morning

Washed away

Wing on wing

Last light of day

Sunset, September 11, 2001